ORDINARY THINGS

TABLE OF CONTENTS

I.

TRIPE	2
THIRD SHIFT	3
FALLING APART	4
THE CHRISTMAS TREE	5
FLAKES OF STONE	6
GRAVITY	7
WALKING	8
LATE MORNING BREAKFAST	9
MEMORY TRICKS	10
MEMORIES OF DOS	11
NO REGRETS	12
THE MORNING CHORE	13
POEM WRITTEN WHILE HOLDING A DOG IN MY LAP	14
AT THE RIGHT HAND OF GOD	15
THE FACE OF GOD	16
BAGGIES	17
THE BIKE RIDE	18
DRIVING TO GENEVA TO CATCH A TRAIN	19
MEADOW LAKE IN WINTER	20
WHILE	21
FOUR	22
FIVE	23
SIX	24
REFLECTIONS	25
PARENTING	27
FATHERS' DAY	28
MONDAY AFTERNOON AT THE AUTO SHOP	29
DAY'S END	30
FADED MEMORY	31
JACKIE	32
THREE-AND-A-HALF HOURS	33
THE OTHER WOMAN	34
GIFT IN THE NIGHT	35
GOLDEN COMB	36

II.

DIABETES	38
THE EVENING RITUAL	39
MAGIC MEDICINE	40
SIXTY-TWO	41

SANCTUARY	42
JUST KILLING TIME	43
TIME	44
ALL NIGHT DINER	45
SMALL VICTORIES	46
THE STARE	47
MEADOW LAKE	48
WAITING	49
LOST PIECES	50
FORM	51
TIMING	52
DRIVEL	53
WHITE	54
BLOCKED	55
SCRATCHINGS	56
THE SIEVE	57
A LETTER TO MYSELF	58
THE MANUSCRIPT	59
REDUNDENCY	60
ENNUI	61
CHECKERS	62
THE DIET	63
MOTION	64
AMAZING GRACE	65
THREE HAIKU	66
SPRING SNOW	67
THE GEESE	68
NO NIRVANA	69
AT WORK IN IBA ZAMBALES	70
THE WALK	71
JACKET WEATHER	72
THE NEW GUY	73
THE IN-BETWEEN	74
TRANSIENCE	75
MAGIC	76
HEADING HOME	77
FOR FAITH	78
ORDINARY THINGS	79
ALONE	80
ANOTHER ONE FOR YOU	81
WHEN YOU'RE NOT NEAR ME	82
AGING BEAUTY	83
HANGING ON	84
PLENTY	85
STEVEN JAMES	86

I.

TRIPE

Thumbnail split to the quick
I pick up the pen
to write these words
What are they for
for self-edification
    to discover some inner thought
    to share myself with the world
The world will never see this
just a lonely few
the people I care about
who care about me
who would never dream of telling me
what tripe it really is

I set my pen aside
to take a sip of coffee
my wife brought me
I read this over
Yes
Tripe

THIRD SHIFT

What do I want to tell you about this Tuesday,
That it's just like any other?
It begins in light and ends in light
and then begins again.
I do not get to share in the wonder
of the opening sky crumbling in the distance.
Instead of birds singing,
I am blessed by the continuing chuck, chuck, chuck
of the sorter in the corner.
And at the end,
I step out under an already bright sun
to calls of "good night," "good night."
My day begins at 3pm
when the dog urges me to take him outside.
And I wonder...
does the rhythm of my sleeping and waking define
the day,
the way the curve of your shoulder and your smile
define my love?

FALLING APART

When I was small
I imagined a world where cars didn't move.
The driver would just focus his mind
on where he wanted to go,
and the world would move under the cars wheels.
I had that feeling today,
driving home from the doctor's office.
I was on the expressway, heading west,
when I noticed that all the eastbound traffic
was at a standstill.
I was in the flow on my side,
going 75,
while the traffic on the other side and the highway
whized past me.
But was I moving?
It was easy to imagine that I was standing still,
maybe sitting in a simulator,
while a screen presented all of this fast, pseudo
reality.
I never took my eyes off the center of the screen.
I made slight adjustments to the steering wheel
as different images popped up before me.
Here I was standing still
while infinity whizzed by
taking me who knows where.
Then I thought -
What if I do move?
What if I move straight through the screen?
Where would I be,
and which side was real?"

And at the doctor's office
the rubber tip of her mallet fell off
as she was testing my reflexes.
As she bent to retrieve it,
she said
"My hammer is falling apart."

THE CHRISTMAS TREE

I lean into the couch.
I become the couch.
As I stare past the tree
to the scene outside our window,
my mind surfs down the leading wave
of all my random thoughts,
and I fall further into the couch.

I live so much of my life between,
between lethargic sorrow,
quiet contemplation,
and,
when she is here,
complete joy.

I stare out the window,
my eyes turning everything into dull sepia tones
like some old photograph
turned face down on the shelf in the closet
and forgotten.

The lights she worked so hard to string on the tree,
just so,
are no longer working,
and I don't know how to fix them.

FLAKES OF STONE

Words are my chosen tool
I use them not as a carpenter building
but as a sculptor taking away,
a chip here,
a flake there,
like birds flying off a telephone wire
revealing nothing but the empty air
they left behind.
I have no plan,
no grand design,
just this impulse,
this need,
to write,
to expose myself,
I guess
to leave behind some image
of myself
as an explanation
or a definition of
of…
see that's the problem.
As I chip away
I don't know what is true.
I'm sure of what is false though.
So I chip away
and hope that what is left,
if anything,
is at least an approximation
of the truth.
I'm searching for my David,
To show me the way to
today,
where I sit
and write
and wonder

GRAVITY

It hurts to stand for more than a few minutes.
Gravity is too much for me now.
My body,
bent forward and to the side,
has let me down.
My mind still walks briskly
and skips and runs.
I remember what it used to feel like
to have my face to the wind.
I can remember rolling down hills
and getting grass stains on my jeans.
And jumping!
I used to jump from rooftops to the ground.
I used to climb.
Now my head is too high above the floor,
and I am dragged down
by the fierce force of careless years.

WALKING

People walk the path around the pond.
As I watch them,
I remember walking,
not this bent hobbling,
walking.
Just a year ago
I could still do it.
What stoops me so now?
Surely not age.
I feel strong still.
I do my exercises and work out on my bike.
But now I cling to a cane.
I can't stand for long.

Look.
Now some people are running.

LATE MORNING BREAKFAST

Breakfast left me fuller than I need to be
Sausages, eggs and potatoes sit in my gut
and weigh me down
This spot
this view
is good enough for now
I'll just sit until the fullness passes
The paper
read
has been folded and put up
no news to take me from this stupor
just reviews of movies that I'll never see
This state of too much comfort
hides the wonder of the moment
I close my eyes and wait for beauty to appear
but held captive by an appetite that knows no
moderation
The afternoon begins without me.

MEMORY TRICKS

Today, over lunch
with my 87-year-old Mother,
I tried to remember the name of the actress
who played the mother of the Carrie Fisher role
in the movie "Postcards from the Edge,"
and Shirley Maclaine just wouldn't come.
Later, when I was no longer thinking about it,
her name suddenly appeared.
More and more
recently
I've come to realize that the library in my mind
has a jumbled up retrieval system.
When I go to check out a book,
it's not where it should be.
Then later, when I'm searching for something else,
I stumble across it
where it's been put on the shelf in the wrong place.
Most of the books are in the right place
and I find them with no difficulty,
but those occasional errors concern me.
If it were only when I'm searching for a book
on a dusty shelf covered with cobwebs
I could understand it,
but it happens with the most frequently requested
books too though.
Or a word I commonly use,
when put on paper or the screen,
suddenly looks foreign to me,
I try and try,
but I can't remember how it should look.
My mind is slowly becoming a patchwork quilt.
And I know that all of this had a point
when I started writing,
but I forget now what it was.

MEMORIES OF DOS

I used to be able to do this,
to crawl across the keys with secret knowings,
creating mysteries of wonder and amazement,
building castles and caverns in the air of my
imagination.
Now I stumble.
I look here and there
and I'm amazed at what mysteries there are for me
today.
I used to be Prometheus
before the ravens came,
fire bringer, wanderer.
I've lost myself
from the lack of use of the old tongue,
and now
there are Windows everywhere,
and I don't know how to see through them.
I download answers for which I have no proper
questions,
and I sigh.
A yesterday I had has not come forward to today,
and I miss it's passing.

NO REGRETS

"Oh – *you're* Walk," she said.
I was in my sunglasses-at-night phase then,
and going by a different name.
"So you're Walk."

We talked until late,
and agreed to see each other the next night.
We did,
and for the next 17 nights as well.
When she left Old Faithful to go home,
we necked in the car all the way to West
Yellowstone
while Eddy drove.

When I went to see her several weeks later
I was no longer Walk;
I was just plain Bill.
That was nearly 45 years ago.
I've been just Bill ever since,

Except when we go to a restaurant.
I always have them put Walk on the waiting list.
"Table for Walk," they say.

THE MORNING CHORE

I didn't need my cap after all.
There was a definite chill
but the sun was bright
and warm.
I stood there,
leash in hand,
behind the community garage,
waiting for him to do his dogly duty
while he just sat,
with an occasional sniff,
tasting the morning air,
admiring the outside world.
I kept watch over the still winter breath
escaping from my nostrils.
He got up several times
and turned his head to the sometimes
passing cars out front,
but always returned,
if not to the same spot,
then to the same pose,
staring at something,
something I couldn't see,
in the near distance.
Finally he turned and turned again
and then he peed
anticlimactically
and we headed back inside
for crate-time
and some treats.

A POEM WRITTEN WHILE HOLDING A DOG IN MY LAP

This devotion
that holds no question
is unique
in a world filled with
promises and
disappointment.
If only I could lie
so assuredly
in the lap of love
and dream
of rabbits and squirrels
and the chewed and worn
cloth bone in the corner.

AT THE RIGHT HAND OF GOD

There used to be a time when I believed
that if I just concentrated hard enough,
I could walk on water,
but I never quite believed it enough
to actually try it.
I'd think that I was Christ reincarnated.
I tried to help other people
(when I remembered to think about it,
and when I wasn't being such an asshole),
I'd try to help other people.
But then I'd always realize -
I'm not Christ.
I always did it for the acclaim,
when there was any,
and there wasn't often enough
as far as I was concerned.
I did it to make my*self* feel good.
That didn't stop me though
from sitting at the right hand of God
and judging the quick and the dead.
I really *was* such a jerk.
And I never gave myself absolution.
I was always right there with the goats.

THE FACE OF GOD

I stood there looking down on her,
with her bruised, cut and stitched face
and her two eyes,
one swollen shut,
swimming in pools of purple.
I listened to her talk about the two operations
she was going to need to repair her broken legs.
She spoke of all her firsts;
her first serious auto accident,
her first ride in an ambulance,
her first time in a helicopter,
her first broken bones,
her first stitches.

Then she laughed.
she spoke of why she felt so blessed,
and I saw the face of God.

BAGGIES

I feel dazed and detached,
maybe a little dizzy.
Did I take too many meds,
or too few?
Taking 14 meds a day
I can't be sure
that they'll always play nicely together.
Or maybe that tuna fish was bad.
No.
I felt this way before lunch.
I sit in my recliner
and push back to a prone position,
a mistake.
I feel it right away,
I feel my body,
the outer shell,
skin and flesh,
becoming transparent.
All that is visible is bones
and innards.
Through my closed eyes
I can see it.
The gravity of the recliner
pulls me in.
I am part of the fabric.

If I knew what caused this
I could put it in baggies
and sell it on the street.

THE BIKE RIDE

Sitting by the camper in the chair Pam brought for me,
I eat ice cream and watch the river
while she and Faith and Wally
all go off on their bicycles.
Suddenly,
I'm blessed by orioles
dipping low to scold us
for disturbing their peace.
Skippy,
oblivious to their complaints,
just prances by my side whining for attention.
Now he's off to explore his territory,
nose down, snuffling across the wet grass.
One of the orioles dives toward him in a mock attack.
He just keeps on searching,
still unaware that he is trespassing.
The sun slowly shows it face through the clouds
and I can feel the temperature start to rise.
My ice cream is all gone.
They don't get back till 45 minutes later.

DRIVING TO GENEVA TO CATCH A TRAIN

Driving down these country roads
I'm blessed by beauty on the way,
sheep and leaves and fields and sky,
a sky that's blue as blue.
I can almost feel bright breezes through my windshield
chilling the crisp loose ends of summer away.
My thoughts drift back to you and you and you.
Where are you now?
I heard you've died,
and you've become a critic.
You're throwing pots on a commune in the north.

And you.
Oh you!
Did you ever learn to play the cello?

I've let my life so drift away
caught in the tides of autumn.

And now I'm at the station,
and they're not here yet.
I wrote their number down,
but, of course, forgot to bring it.

MEADOW LAKE IN THE WINTER

The lake is covered over with snow,
so it's hard to tell
where the water ends
and the shore begins.

Nothing moves
except for the grasses
where the wind goes.
I always wonder –
why don't they sway in unison?
Instead they bob and weave
on their brittle stalks
in a dance of opposition –
you go this way,
I'll go that.

Two people are walking
the path around the lake.
Now they stop to photograph
the trees on the other side.
Now done,
They head up toward the parking lot.
How can they think
the lake they take with them
is any match for all this bright beauty?

WHILE

While my Faith
sits in the kitchen
talking to Linda
on the phone,
I sit here at the keyboard
struggling,
huffing and puffing
over the keys,
hoping that somehow,
someway,
I'll be able to trip across
some kind of inspiration.

All I can come up with
is empty.
There is no fullness here.
Blah.
Blah.
Blah.
Nothing.

FOUR

"I want to eat the woald," he says so absolutely.
"I'm gonna eat cars an..."
"If you eat my car,
we'll have to walk."
'O*tay*! I won't.
I'm gonna eat trucks,
big trucks,
an roads
an signs,
an the grass...'
He sticks his head out the window
"I'm gonna eat you trees!"
He pulls his head back inside.
"An I'm gonna eat the sky
an the moon
an the stars
an the ho univewse.
An I'm gonna eat people
an *poop*
an I'm gonna drink *pee*!'
He has a malicious, I'm-a-naughty-boy grin.
With his head out the window again.
"I'm gonna eat you dog!"

I can't even remember when I was going to eat the world.

FIVE

Twenty-eight of the 30 computer stations are
occupied.
It's a beautiful, breezy day
and I wonder what's driven us all inside.
For me,
it's a chance to write with no distractions,
but then – no – that's not really it.
It's a chance to be out of the apartment
while Faith watches our youngest grandson.
He's no real trouble,
but lately we've been playing the puppy game.
Using nothing but our imaginations.
we spot and collect baby animals.
Over and over and over again.
I love his imagination,
but this constant having to be engaged wears me
out.
Today
Faith is teaching him Go Fish,
and I'm here at the library
hiding out.

SIX

As I write this on a napkin found in the glove box,
the sun is bright against the windshield
(which really does shield)
and the car pulses in the cold winter wind.
I am toasty-warm inside,
waiting for Jordan.
When school ends,
he will see me here as usual,
and come to the car for another afternoon
adventure.
Will it be his house and video games?
(with me just watching)
Will it be for my apartment and go fish
or the puppy game?
No.
Today it will be the video store and the library.
I have things to do,
and for a candy bar Jordan will let me do them.
(but we'll probably play I spy on the way)
Forty-five minutes to go
and two more cars have pulled up.
(soon they'll be lined up out into the street)
I am always first.
I love him that much.

REFLECTIONS

I think I was six
or seven
when I figured out
that she was going to die someday.
I cried and cried,
and begged her not to die,
not ever.

She was very bright,
still is.
It's not as though she's dead yet.
but she was always a little scatter-brained, too.
She would get lost easily.
She was, is, very forgetful.
Once when she picked me up in Minnesota
after I'd graduated from high school,
we went by train to D.C.
Our new home was in Bethesda, Maryland,
not far from there.
She and Dad and my two sisters
had been living there for about three months
while I finished school where we used to live.
Anyway,
we were in different cars.
She had a sleeper,
and I didn't.
I just slept leaning back as far as my seat would go,
So,
in the morning I heard the conducter
announcing that we were coming into D.C.
I went to look for her,
and I couldn't find her.
I got off the train,
still looking around,
and she just wasn't there.
A little over an hour later
I saw *him* coming through the concourse
looking all around.

When he saw me,
he came over,
shook my hand,
and led me out to the car where she was waiting.
She had forgotten all about me.
She had gotten off the train
at the Silver Spring stop,
which was closest to home.
She'd walked to his waiting car with her suitcase
and got in.
Then he asked, where's Bill.

As I got older
our relationship changed;
I grew more apart from her.
She would always apologize to me
for all the mistakes she thought she'd made
while raising me.
She *made* mistakes,
but I'm the person I am today
because of me
as much as because of her.
I made more mistakes than she did.

I will always love her.
She moves into the retirement community on
Monday.
Please don't die, mommy.
Please don't ever die.

PARENTING

Becoming a parent turned me into a walking oxymoron,
I remember sitting at dinner one night
when our twin girls were teasing our young son Joe.
The more they teased,
the madder he got.
Finally, tired of it all,
I slammed my fist on the table and said,
"Damn it, Joe, getting mad doesn't do any good at all!"
Later,
when I told a neighbor about this,
she said,
"I know what you mean.
when I caught Gregory hitting Jessica yesterday,
I grabbed him by the arm,
swatted his bottom,
and said,
'Gregory!
We don't hit people!'"

FATHERS DAY

He was standing in the kitchen in his robe.
As I was leaving,
I went to hug him.
He held his hand up –stop!
We don't do that in my generation he said.
His father never hugged him.
I always thought they both were wrong.

He was hard driven to achieve at any cost,
to his health, his family.
He nearly died from a bleeding ulcer,

But I did love him.

He called me every Saturday.
He always supported me.
Those were his gifts to me.
I also got some of his craziness
and his temper.

I always hugged my son,
but, no matter how I tried,
and I didn't try often enough,
I never was a better father then he had been.

MONDAY AFTERNOON AT THE AUTO SHOP

Watching Jim's hands,
oil-streaked and rough,
I am lost in the realization
that, I, intentionally
and with malice,
would've broken the door assembly
before figuring out how to take it off properly.
It's the knowing that I lack;
what can be forcibly pulled out,
and what needs to be unscrewed,
and where, exactly, are the screws anyway?
Twenty minutes later,
I leave with the rear, driver's side window back in place.

I never have been handy.
My father always told me so.
It's not his fault, though.
I always believed him.

DAY'S END

Where has the day gone
I meant to do so much
but everything got away from me
like boats with lost rudders
I wandered aimlessly as a dog in heat
searching for my next satisfaction
until no satisfaction was left to me
and I headed home empty-handed
The sun is low in the sky
and I have so little to show for the day
no metals upon this chest
no gold star placed on this day's date
Do others end their days like this
seeking some accounting
some measure of the day's worth
Are they satisfied
or oblivious
I wonder
Regardless
when darkness settles down
I'll go to sleep

FADED MEMORY

You with the yellow hair
falling like sun-soaked raindrops on your shoulders,
how,
with brushstrokes of blue, green and gold
you painted childhood
and its end.
Your precociousness taught teachers
what art could be.
And yet,
you gave it up you said,
with all seriousness,
to learn to play the cello.
You astonished me with your effrontery
and your talents.
"I'll sleep with you," you said
"but you'll have to court me."
When the time came,
you wanted me to promise that I'd ride with you
on the bus back from the hotel,
and I wouldn't.
I'd gladly have ridden with you though with no
promise.

Your beauty was too demanding,
more an empty promise than a fact.
I think of you from time to time
without regret,
just wondering what kind of life you've had,
just wondering that's all.

JACKIE

"Prepare to be dazzled."
she said,
the day of *that* party
so many Halloweens ago.

Somewhere below the need for defenses,
beneath the fear of hurts,
inside the whelmed and vulnerable heart,
there is a darkness that waits for light.
And, sometimes,
in that waiting,
there is comfort
from our endless passings through
and empty auld lang synes,
as we are drawn like moths to flame
to flashes in the night.

"Prepare to be dazzled."
she said.
But her warning came too late.

THREE-AND-A-HALF HOURS

Sitting in the car
in the rain
listening to the radio
I wonder what it's all about,
all this coming and going
with little time
for comforting
or for loving.
I miss you
leaning into my side
on the couch,
my arm around you
pulling you close.
Eyes closed,
you slip into slumber
and I know
I'm home.
The rain lets up
and it's time
to get back to work.

Three-and-a-half hours
To go.

THE OTHER WOMAN

First.
You must know
that I do not love you less
(but more,
if that is possible).
But when I see her,
she fills my heart
with sunshine
and with daisies
(her favorite flowers).
When she dances across my memory,
I am caught again
in the net of her sweet love.
I can never let her go,
and I hope that you will understand,
but when I see her smiling out
through your eyes,
or catch a remembered gesture
or expression,
I can never forget,
and will always love
the woman that you are now
and the girl that I met
on her 19th birthday.

GIFT IN THE NIGHT

There are no defenses between us now,
but comfortable familiarity.
I lie down by the side of love
that holds remembered in this pause a kiss,
and while I dream a dream that thoughts may hide
of stolen moments from the warmth you give,
I clutch the rising tide of sentiment,
this all so frequent moment's cozy bliss.
You hold me to a better self
than I alone could ever offer to
a world that's traced by blessings from your touch,
that's given freely to my worn delight.
I marvel once more at the precious gift
and cherish these close moments in the night

GOLDEN COMB

Give me now my golden comb
as I the wide-eyed cock do crow
to break the early morning's misting
with my shallow-seeded song.

Give me now this simple pleasure,
I the cock to crow at dawn.
While others in their beds lie dreaming,
come, you and I shall lie alone.

Hold me now. A wondrous treasure
lies within your arms I've found.
Share with me this moment's madness
of desire that's been unbound.

Kiss me now, and be for giving
As I know that you can be.
Touch me now. Life's for the living.
Come and live your life with me.

Still you lie. This tender moment
Shall be noticed by the spheres.
Cherish me as I shall cherish.
Be my lover all these years.

II.

DIABETES

I tap the bottom of my bare left heel
to the disjointed, thumping rhythm
of some song or another
almost without recognition
of its being mine.

How long before it's gone?

THE EVENING RITUAL

I pick them out
one by one,
one for this.
two for that.
three for the other.

I am sane again,
and the diseased blood
tracing the path of mortality
through the hallways
of my heart.
sings!

MAGIC MEDICINE

Four in the morning
two at night
then I can lean back
into a more comfortable reality
The world seems closer
less cluttered
more relaxed
Everything has a purpose
though purposes elude me.
I go through my sunshine days
in an unfocused haze
and find a kind of peace

SIXTY-TWO

With parchment fingers that smell of long ago
I grasp at shadows of yesterday's tomorrows that
never came.
Now I drive too slowly
and young men on motorcycles curse me as they
pass.

SANCTUARY

Sitting in the swing
on grandma and poppy's front porch
trying to keep my bare feet from scraping the rough
concrete,
eating a tomato fresh picked from the garden,
with the seedy juices running down my face
onto my shirt,
I wonder if it's time
to go for the cows in the far field,
and I ponder the mysteries of the woods
without fear.

JUST KILLING TIME

I throw away handfuls of sand,
not even aware of the phases of the moon.
I've heard the slapping of the sea's attack and
retreat
without recognizing the sound of my own final
breath.
And while I sit here,
just killing time,
time races on ahead
killing me.

TIME

Time makes no sense to me,
or, at least, time in the past doesn't.
All my memories are episodic;
they are not linear.
I have a chicken and egg kind of memory.
I remember this and that,
but not which came first.

ALL NIGHT DINER

I live in the spaces between the everyday and the
eternal,
where God exists in the weeks old dustball in the
corner.
Joy and sorrow are left in my never full,
never quite empty,
bowl of 40 hour weeks
with no weekends separating them
from oblivion.
My life is an all night diner
with no waitresses on duty.
I help myself to the coffee.

SMALL VICTORIES

I would love to go strolling
through the mall naked,
but maybe I'll just dye my hair blue instead,
if my wife will let me.
She's already said
I can't get any more tattoos.
So maybe
I'll just write a peculiar poem instead
and let it go at that.

I celebrate such small victories.

THE STARE

You sat behind me
at another table.
"I don't want you staring at me
while I'm journaling," you said,
as though my stare
could stop your pen dead in its tracks.
So you write, and I sit here
gunning down strangers
with my eyes.

MEADOW LAKE

Ripples
reflecting light
shine across the middle of the lake
while two women
at the table in front of me
share hand cream
and talk tentatively against the noise.

I hear a bird singing.
I wonder where it is,
or if it's even real.

WAITING

So I've already checked my e-mail five times today
and it's only two o'clock.
Faith's been busy almost all day
and now she's at a doctor's appointment.
Skippy and the white pitcher in the
corner with the fake flowers in it
keep me company.
He sleeps in my lap peacefully.
My leg cramps,
but I don't want to move it and disturb him.
If I did decide to disturb him though,
I'd get up and see if anybody's e-mailed me yet.

LOST PIECES

I don't remember yesterday.
Was I even alive.
I know I got up at 6:00AM
to take the dog out.
I must've taken my pills,
in the morning,
again at night.
It's a puzzlement.

If I am the result
of everything that's
ever happened to me,
I'm losing pieces of me.

FORM

He comes off the slide into the deep end.
He can't really swim,
but he can dog paddle ferociously
He makes it to the side and climbs up the ladder.

While I stand here
picturing the crawl
or the breaststroke
and wishing he had proper form,
he rushes back to the top of the slide.

He has no style,
but he's having lots of fun.

TIMING

Too many times,
when the poem is finished,
I keep on writing.

DRIVEL

Like a self-test on a printer,
I sit down at the keyboard to write.
Instead of a prescribed bit of text
or a preset pattern,
what comes out is unpredictable.
Its quality is erratic,
often poor, sometimes just passable,
and, very rarely, quite good.

If only I could tell the difference.

WHITE

I hate this empty sheet of paper!
I am bored by it.
Why does it so define my day?

BLOCKED

My pen is running out of ink
I heard her say at the next table.
She was writing something down for a friend.
I was trying to write a poem.
My pen was full,
But my mind was empty.
Surrounded by life
I had nothing but dead thoughts
And a head full of dust kittens and cobwebs.
I stepped outside
Hoping the chill wind would invigorate me.
It only made me cold.

SCRATCHINGS

Bogged down by sensation
Imagination's overwhelmed
I try to write inside this cocoon of sight and sound
But all that comes is a muffled mellowness
I'm too here to put it down
Just a few feeble scratchings and I'm done

THE SIEVE

This writing what I think at every moment
Fills the page
But lacks a lasting value
Like a picture of a cloud in motion
That just shows gray against a lighter gray
I cannot do this moment justice
My pen is empty as a sieve of water.

A LETTER TO MYSELF

I wrote several things today,
none of them very good,
but I wrote.

THE MANUSCRIPT

"Something edgier" he said
"Someone else"
He did not tell me who

I speak slowly
never raise my voice
but there's still a Voice
It's not just mental masturbation
This pen
this paper
I stain each page with who I am
but my dusty words lie fallow in a field of hope

REDUNDENCY

Brain freeze -
the sign in the window at Saxby's Coffee touts.
Brain freeze?
Mine's frozen most of the time already.

ENNUI

The early afternoon sun
comes through our window
and settles on the artificial flowers
on the sway-shelved bookcase,
while the small wooden giraffe
looks away, disinterestedly.
I just sit and wonder
when the coffee's going to be ready.
And the large, blue exercise ball,
not quite in the center of the room,
sits in a pleasant pool of sunlight.

CHECKERS

I hate playing checkers by myself.
I get bored,
and I always lose.

THE DIET

I am tired of being fat.
I eat less and less,
but still it hasn't gone away.
I don't understand it.
It's been nearly a week.

MOTION

Everything is moving but the ground
I am lost in motion
hypnotized by ripples and the grasses in the wind
I do not have the answer to the question of today
I sit here anchored in this chair with wheels
and dream a day that never ends

AMAZING GRACE

A maze among the evergreens,
and I am lost.
Now I'm found.
Amazing Grace
under a bright, sun-burst sky.

THREE HAIKU

Skeletal fingers
Hold green's promise to the sky.
Snow falls on the ground.

A single bird flies.
Winter's sky is wide and deep.
The bird disappears.

Dirty snow lines streets.
Dingy clouds slump on the sky.
Everything is grey.

SPRING SNOW

What do I want,
here on this couch,
in this moment,
the world outside the window dancing
green against the snow-puffed clouds?
What do I want?
Just this,
just here,
just now.

THE GEESE

In the distance,
two Canadian geese.
one stationary,
resting on the ground,
the other foraging for food
among the grasses
underneath the trees.

Now one flies away.

NO NIRVANA

When I try to keep my mind empty,
things keep nibbling at the edges.
How can I find nirvana in this fractured cup?

AT WORK IN IBA ZAMBALES

While others work
in the hot sun,
all I am good for
is sitting in the shade
and drinking coconut milk
and coffee.

While the sea rushes to the shore
and the wind blows
and blows,
a fly lands on my hand
and is not afraid.

THE WALK

A solitary winged creature
traipses across the heads of flowers
that grow wild at the edge of the water,
As I,
like the baby in the carriage that we pass,
am wheeled slowly about the pond.
And I wonder:
Is that gently flying creature lonely, too?

JACKET WEATHER

Resting in the sun,
slumped back in my chair,
eyes closed,
an early spring breeze
reminds me that a winter left
not so long ago,
and it's still jacket weather.

THE NEW GUY

Alone,
in this company of strangers,
first night jitters,
third shift.
What's ahead?
Can I make one more notch
in the handle of my aging dreams?
Or will I walk
Empty-hearted into the morning sun?
Nothing but frayed twine
and loose ends
in my knot of expectations.

THE GOD OF THE IN-BETWEEN

I believe in God,
the God of the in-between.
He exists somewhere between chance and
circumstance.
He is not a protector
but a comforter and a strength giver,
the constant knowing that I am not alone.
He is always there
between me and my times of greatest need.
And in my celebrations,
He shields me from my self-absorption.
Somewhere between proofs and insufficiencies,
I find faith.

TRANSIENCE

I stare at a spot on the walk.
People walk through it
and I see them clearly
while they're in it.
After they pass,
my peripheral vision
holds them for a while.

Gradually they fade
and then are gone.

MAGIC

Just for a moment
I saw something written in the trees.
I couldn't read it,
but it was there.
Now there are only trunks and branches.

HEADING HOME

Like a mint too long on the tip of my tongue,
the thought of you is there,
just there,
burning,
stinging with a delight that dares me to let it go,
but I can't.
Just a minute longer,
just a moment,
and then,
there.
It's gone.
Now I'm faced with the reality of the long drive
home

FOR FAITH

Eyes brown as wet wood in a rain...
and a smile, such a smile!
And touches soft as grass.
You move across my thoughts in random patterns
that cannot be captured.
I do love you so.
And if I did not have a life to live with you
my heart would break.
And I would miss your
eyes brown as wet wood in a rain...
and your smile.
And I would miss your love.

ORDINARY THINGS

My days are filled with ordinary things
I get up
I lie down
I walk
I sit
I read
I rest
Doing nothing but filling time
And space
Another day
So inconsequential
So filled with nothing but your love

ALONE

A blind-striped shadow
hangs against the wall.
It holds the profiles of Nefertiti
and the singing pig.
On this side of the shadow
I sit
surrounded by things:
furniture, rugs, assorted books
and pictures and bric-a-brac.
What does all of this have to do with me?
Where are you, my love?
When will you be home?

ANOTHER ONE FOR YOU

I love you in the sunlight,
moon light,
star light,
really *any* light at all.

But especially in the quiet dark,
when you cup my hand beneath your throat
and fall asleep.

I listen to your breathing,
in and out and in and out,
and dream a past where I've been kinder to you.

WHEN YOU"RE NOT NEAR ME

When you're not with me
I need to hold you near
Remembering your voice
your touch
is like trying to hold the wind
My love for you is constant as birdsong in the
morning
I need you like the air I breathe
When are you coming back?

AGING BEAUTY

She sits with lyrics and her glass
and sings and sings.
As the record plays
she keeps pace
intent and beautiful.
Her voice is not as
strong as it once was,
but it's still my favorite sound.

HANGING ON

I found you early
and hung on
That is my salvation
you are always with me
in my heart
in my mind
When my thoughts leave your side
They always come back
You are my soul's magnet

PLENTY

No reason now
for loneliness
or pain
All my nights are filled
with gentle breathing,
And when I wake
I know that she'll be there.
No shucked off husk for tossing
I am green and golden
in a field of accidental plenty.

STEVEN JAMES

I thought of Steven this afternoon.
I was reading Anne Lamott's <u>Bird by Bird.</u>
and something made me think of him,
and I sobbed,
not for long,
probably for no longer than he'd lived.

Faith had to leave the hospital empty,
nothing in her womb,
nothing in her arms.
I cried for her
almost as much as I did for him.

Made in the USA
Charleston, SC
15 October 2016